EFFECTIVE
PRESENTATIONS

Also by Marc Zimmer in Sphere Books:

A–Z of Small Business
Is Your Business Really Successful?

EFFECTIVE
PRESENTATIONS

Marc Zimmer

Sphere Reference

SPHERE BOOKS LIMITED

Penguin Books Ltd, 27 Wrights Lane, London W8 5TZ (Publishing and Editorial)
and Harmondsworth, Middlesex, England (Distribution and Warehouse)
Viking Penguin Inc., 40 West 23rd Street, New York, New York 10010, USA
Penguin Books Australia Ltd, Ringwood, Victoria, Australia
Penguin Books Canada Ltd, 2801 John Street, Markham, Ontario, Canada L3R 1B4
Penguin Books (NZ) Ltd, 182–190 Wairau Road, Auckland 10, New Zealand

First published by Sphere Books Ltd 1987

TRADE
MARK

Made and Printed in Great Britain by
Cox and Wyman Ltd, Reading, Berks
Filmset in Linotron Times by
Rowland Phototypesetting Ltd, Bury St Edmunds, Suffolk

Contents

Acknowledgements

For research: S.B.
For audio-visual material: A. Saville Group.

Introduction

The objective of this book is to develop skills in effective presentations. The aim of it is to give guidance on how to achieve that objective.

Contrary to widely held views, anyone can make an effective presentation. However, we have all seen and felt embarrassed by speakers who make a poor presentation. When does this occur? If we reflect a moment

- it could be a conference
- it could be an in-house company meeting
- it could be a training course.

There are many other situations in which we have seen speakers and perhaps *been* speakers in obvious difficulties!

To be successful you must begin by accepting that it is an unnatural situation to speak to any group. Whether it is large or small, to improve your delivery *you must have the commitment to develop your speaking technique.*

The best speakers I have met are not 'born' to it, but are people who prepare thoroughly, practise their delivery and gain experience by actually doing it! *Everyone* suffers from pre-speaking nerves which can vary uncontrollably from venue to venue. However, there are techniques, described in this book, to help *you* keep your composure and deliver a more effective presentation.

PART I

1   The Commitment to Develop

I want to be good

O.H.P.

We will begin by considering two contrasting case histories.

Case History 1: Mr Smith

Mr Smith knocked gently on the Director's door.

'Come in.'

Following the prompt response, Smith moved nervously into the room towards the large, well-polished mahogany

2

desk behind which loomed the domineering, larger-than-life Director, Mr Bigwig of the Northern Region.

'Sit down, please,' said Mr Bigwig. 'We've had a memo from Head Office stating that Jones is to be transferred to another area.'

How does that affect me? wondered Mr Smith. But not for long, as Mr Bigwig told him, 'As you know, Mr Jones is our area speaker for colleges and industry groups. He is leaving. Therefore Head Office want *you* to take over as speaker.'

A lightning bolt of fear struck Mr Smith at the horrifying prospect of addressing groups of people and he stammered, 'But, Mr Bigwig, I haven't any experience of public speaking and I don't think I could possibly do it.'

Mr Bigwig was not interested at all. He told Smith that he would reply in the affirmative to Head Office and that before Mr Jones left he should go with him to his next talk, watch him and gain experience.

For days Mr Smith was in a dilemma, tossing things over in his mind. When he accompanied Mr Jones to his final talk, things became even worse. Mr Jones's performance was relaxed and confident. He sat jauntily on the side of a desk at the front of the group and talked very knowledgeably almost without notes! He handled questions comfortably, with an air of confidence.

Mr Smith was shattered at the prospect of taking over as speaker from Mr Jones and knew that he had no chance of matching Mr Jones's confident delivery. He entered a deep depression. He felt he had no alternative. He must resign from the company.

Case History 2: Mr Overrun

Mr Overrun put down the telephone, smiled with satisfaction and told his office colleague of his next public speaking engagement. He then began discussing the title of the talk he had been requested to give.

Later Mr Overrun's colleague tried in vain to intervene, but Mr Overrun dashed from one part of the office to the other swooping on bits of previous talks and amassing piles of paper to aid his talk.

'How long are you speaking for?'

'One hour,' Overrun replied.

The day of his talk came and the confident Mr Overrun packed everything available into his talk with little regard for timing or the structure of the presentation. Or, indeed, any regard whatsoever as to what the audience actually wanted!

Mid-afternoon, several days later, Mr Overrun enters the office after returning from his speaking engagement.

'How did it go?' asks Mr Overrun's colleague, smiling in anticipation.

'Terrible!' came the depressing reply.

'But I thought . . .'

'I never reached my best material. My introduction took twenty minutes. The next speaker was getting irritated because I overran fifteen minutes, so I just had to sit down.'

Mr Overrun's colleague sympathised and tried discussing with him why the talk had gone so badly wrong.

You have read of the contrasting plight of the two speakers in the case histories. Both are true stories. Mr Overrun continues to present his talks in a confident and pleasant manner, but will always have difficulties with timing until he can rigidly monitor his progress during his talks. Meanwhile Mr Smith was going to resign from his company. He could not cope with the prospect of giving talks. You might think this reaction extreme, but I can assure you it's true. *I am Mr Smith!*

In ten years I have progressed from the situation described to you in Case History 1 to now being on a national speakers' panel and writing this book. I now speak all over the United Kingdom. I am not being pompous and many readers will have never heard me speak and probably never will. The point is that I can convey to you, through the medium of this book, my experiences.

Some of my ideas will assist you; some you may wish to discard.

We will begin by turning back to my plight when faced with the prospect of replacing Mr Jones as the new area speaker. I could not raise the courage to quit. I needed the money and my wife was pregnant. I *had* to tackle the issue. Having resolved to do so, I needed to understand the problem.

Understanding the Problem

The problem was readily apparent to me. Mr Jones was confident, experienced and a *natural* talker, full of conversation. I was a poor conversationalist, certainly no orator, hampered by a northern accent. I didn't know the material and had no experience whatsoever at giving talks. Forty to love down – but not out!

My commitment was that I needed to continue.

What did I do next? I did not know any other speakers to discuss my problem with. Mr Jones had left the area, but I knew we had a control contact point at Head Office for all area speakers. I knew that because they were the people who had given me the job.

One telephone call to Head Office changed everything.

Useful Techniques

I explained that I was the new area speaker replacing Mr Jones and wondered if they could help me with my first talk and outlined the topic to them.

Much to my surprise the man on the telephone was actually extremely helpful! He said he had comprehensive notes on the topic in question and also visual aids. Had I used these before? He went on to explain that he had charts available for wall mounting and also some transparencies for use with a projector and a screen.

I eagerly awaited his parcel . . .

The package arrived and I studied the contents. They looked good and I felt a glimmer of hope. Although I was mystified by the transparencies, ideas came flooding in.

- What if I put up two of these huge charts on a blackboard or something? I could talk with this support for possibly ten minutes. After all, it would be a small group and they could see the charts.

- What if I condensed the comprehensive notes into a précis that I could use for discussion with the group and also as a hand-out?
- What about telephoning the venue organiser and seeing if they had some sort of machine that would project the transparencies. Again, it would be different from Mr Jones's talk!

I began to feel quite enthusiastic. One thing was for sure: I might still be hopeless, but my presentation would certainly be different.

- What about going to the reference library to see if there were any articles on public speaking that would help?

Projecting Oneself

I tried to visualise the room. I had the obvious advantage of being there before with Mr Jones. The room was small but so was the group. That should be satisfactory.

I then tried to visualise the charts pinned up on the wall at the front, visible to all the group.

I had confirmed with the organiser that an overhead projector would be available. This would be a difficulty in that I had no experience with this type of machine, but the organiser had told me on the phone that it was easy to use.

Finally, and most importantly, I tried to visualise myself in the room at the front speaking to the group.

What should I wear? Should I sit like Jones or stand? If I stood, should I keep still or move about? I could not decide, so I let things drift around in my mind over the next few days.

The day of the talk loomed nearer. I had visited the library and located some background reading which related mainly to famous speakers (for instance, politicians) and, although they were interesting, they did not give a lot of help for a talk at my level.

I revisualised the room. I would stand and move around a

little. I would dress smartly in a suit in which I felt good. Yes, that would be my plan . . .

My First Talk

I arrived a few minutes early and met the organiser. We had coffee in a small ante-room and then moved into the main room where I was to speak. *My first mistake!* The room was already set up and the audience waiting in their chairs! I had no chance to position anything, either visuals or seating arrangements.

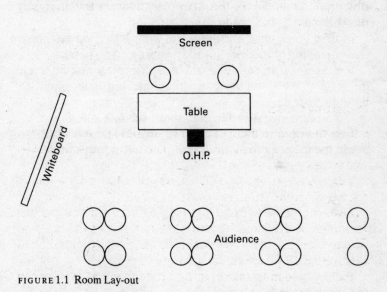

FIGURE 1.1 Room Lay-out

The room lay-out was as illustrated in Figure 1.1. I put my transparencies, talk notes, hand-outs on the table. Quickly, with the organiser's help, I pinned up the charts on a whiteboard which was located at right-angles to the audience! I felt embarrassed at carrying out last-minute tasks in front of the group waiting patiently for me to begin. Everyone seemed to be watching me.

On the positive side, I did find, however, that I had no time to sit and build up nerves, as the organiser quickly introduced me and I was off!

I can still remember stammering through my opening. The words I had written down seemed so alien when spoken. I quickly moved to the wall charts. I felt more comfortable talking through this section, but of course the audience were not. The charts were to the side of the group, which caused a lot of shuffling about.

The hand-outs went down well. However, I found that when using the transparencies they were projected straight behind me and I tended to obscure the screen. That is, I obscured the screen for those people who were watching and not still reading the hand-out!

I found questions difficult to deal with. It was hard to grasp their meaning immediately and I was slow to respond.

It was soon at an end – the end of my first presentation. I felt deflated at the thought of my bungling, but determined to have another go.

Despite my negative feelings about the talk, the organiser felt that the group had got good value and learned a lot! He asked me to speak to another group in one month's time!

2   Types of Presentation

Will the type of presentation you give always be the same?

No. You must reflect on this. Think back to my first talk. I was fortunate in that it was given to a small group in a fairly informal situation.

Imagine a totally different situation, say, giving a presentation from a platform to an audience of two hundred people! You may wince at the prospect and no wonder. It could be an awful experience to encounter this as your very first effort. Unless you are very skilled or lucky or both, it could put you off for life.

Many people shun 'platforms' all their business life and yet they have powerful individual messages that could be conveyed to their less experienced colleagues. Not everyone has the opportunity to gain experiences of different countries for example, or different sales experiences, and many would benefit from *your* thoughts conveyed in an effective manner.

Now if you know that almost certainly one day you will be asked to 'say a few words', then why not try to arrange a few *low-profile talks* to small groups to prepare your way?

The Event

Begin by asking:

- What is the event?
- What is the nature and purpose of the event?
- Who will be in the audience?
- What is their level of experience?
- Will you be the only speaker?
- Who is organising the event?
- Why are they having the event at all?

This type of questioning may seem basic but it is an essential process for you to go through. It is essential, because it is the beginning from which you will frame the matrix of your talk.

It's really no use at all planning a roving-around style of presentation that you might use in a training situation as a group leader if you are likely to find yourself anchored to the spot by a lectern and lassoed by a neck microphone! You won't be able to move more than a few inches either way.

OK, so you have considered the event. Most likely it will fall into one of the following categories:

- an in-company presentation to the board
- a talk to a small group
- a training session
- a conference
- an after-dinner talk.

We have already discussed a small group situation in our first case history. Refresh your memory by restudying the ideas used and the pitfalls encountered.

You can always be certain of one thing: if there is a chance something will go wrong, *it will!*

Because of your individual qualities, there will be one or more presentations that you will prefer; certainly one or more that you will like least. I suggest that the after-dinner talk is the most difficult, unless you are a natural at telling humorous stories.

It all depends on:

- your personality
- your style
- your material
- your preparation
- your rehearsal
- your experience.

An In-company Presentation

Presentation to the board.

Here we are considering a presentation to a very small group, but this can be quite a gruelling situation. No one wants to make a fool of himself or herself in front of people with whom you will continue to work. You could be chatting quite cosily over coffee before the meeting and five minutes later an erstwhile 'friend' of yours is trying to shoot you down and score points in front of the boss!

How many times have you seen your colleagues caught out and embarrassed? How can you overcome this?

The answer is simple. Be well prepared.

Because it is in-company, you *could* be quite casual about presentation. *Don't be.*

- Do have a reserve of information and statistics.
- Do be brief to begin with, holding back on your reserve.
- You will feel comfortable in the knowledge that you have plenty of back-up material tucked away and concealed neatly in that plain-backed folder beneath your outline meeting notes.

Don't bother with funny stories. Everyone is busy at work. Be direct and to the point.

- *Be professional.*

'I am reporting on sales for the Northern Region. This last quarter we achieved our budgeted sales of £— and in fact I am pleased to report . . .'

That's a good direct opening.

If you have a lot of statistics to present consider using one of the following:

- *a hand-out* – pass this around to colleagues so that they can look at the figures whilst you talk over the data
- *an overhead projector* – to display more clearly the information on a screen
- *a flip chart* – on which you can write key statistics.

Occasionally you may wish to illustrate a new product and this can be done more effectively by the use of:

- colour photographs
- 35 mm slide projection on to a screen
- a video tape (although this is usually expensive to produce).

The video may be the most expensive, but it will certainly hold people's attention.

A Training Session

Here you could be fulfilling the role of course director or acting as a lecturer.

As a course director your presentation will probably be confined to the opening up of the course and a closing session. What style will that take?

Often it's usual simply to sit at the front of the group addressing them from a prepared course outline and giving points on administration. You could employ the technique of asking the participants to introduce themselves in turn and give a short brief on their individual backgrounds. In that way they become the presenters – and you simply sit back and relax!

As a course director, the closing session of a course is very important in that you are endeavouring to pull everything together and often trying to obtain feedback on the course. Here your style must be relaxed and coaxing.

As a training session lecturer, your presentation will be totally different.

Here you are being paid to convey some knowledge whilst at the same time encouraging participation by means of questions and discussion of points.

You *must* be familiar with the material; if you are not, then the students will soon sense this and give you a very hard time!

Try to use visual aids – whiteboards, hand-outs, an overhead projector – and exercises. Although you are only addressing a group of students, you will still suffer from nerves. Sometimes you will feel very apprehensive, but you must get stuck in and try to move about. Moving about, towards and around the students will help you break the ice and soon you will relax. Timing is important. If it is a long session, make sure that you all have a five-minute break, say, every hour. Also keep the room well ventilated.

Video is a powerful aid which can be used in two ways:

- as a film outlining key points
- as a means of self-study by incorporating video-camera facilities.

The first use is a powerful medium for messages. The second will frighten many course participants. They are not used to it and may well freeze up. However, it can be instructive and fun if *you* can handle the situation correctly.

- Try not to use an 'outsider' to operate the video camera. *Use it in a static position.*
- Put yourself on *first*, then draw lots.
- Remember that people are all individuals.
- Encourage the person filmed to talk through it later on; but *do not ask the remaining group members to criticise!* This is terribly destructive of the atmosphere you are trying to promote.

In general, try to encourage discussion of any controversial points – you won't always be right! If you get a really difficult question that you can't answer, be prepared to say, 'That's a very good question. I can't give you an immediate answer, but I will come back to you later.'

A Conference

There are conferences and there are conferences. You must get the feel of what is required.

- Is it the national annual conference of a certain group and you are there as one of many speakers?
- Is it a conference on a specialised theme and you are requested to give a specialist input?
- Is it a conference of your own company and you are requested to speak on a section of the corporate plan and performance to date?

How you tackle the presentation will depend on the venue. For certain, your mobility will be restricted. If there are other speakers actually present on the platform whilst you talk, this is an added difficulty. No matter how good you are, you will feel the audience's attention straying towards the other speakers. They may be mentally identifying them, thinking about their own talks to come, or about the content of the talks that have already been.

Even if the conference is fairly formal, try to use some form of visual aid to break up your talk. Your style of presentation will be vastly different from that in the training session environment. The audience will be expecting a more 'rigid' presentation and you can be very effective by presenting yourself in an efficient and business-like manner.

Question time is usually easier to handle. Probably it will be an open forum session at the end of the talks with all speakers present.

You might be a single speaker on a specialised topic with an audience of, say, sixty to a hundred people in a conference-style setting.

I find this much easier. Although you will probably be speaking for much longer, you will have a lot more freedom and a lot more *control* over the situation.

Just how quickly things warm up will most certainly depend on *you*!

- You have to project yourself enthusiastically.
- You have to seem pleased to be there even if you are nervous.
- You have to gain and *maintain* the audience's attention.

In this situation you have no restrictions on what the other speakers might be doing and you have plenty of 'platform' space. Try, therefore, to use perhaps two or even three differing types of visual aid during your presentation. This will help you keep audience attention and is particularly useful if you are talking for one hour or more. Later in this book we will examine in some detail the use of visual aids.

The in-company conference is a different matter. This time you will most likely be required to give a much shorter presentation. You don't need to move at all. Just put over the facts quickly and efficiently. Don't tell funny stories – but don't look like a 'dummy'. Try to smile. After all, these people are your colleagues.

If you have a lot of data to put over in a short time, a particularly effective way is to use 35 mm slides. You can stand back while they all watch the screen and you can rattle through your delivery with little attention focused upon you.

An After-dinner Talk

I feel this is the hardest type of presentation to make, but this is not much consolation if you have to do it!

Why is this so?

Visualise the scenario:

- it's probably a smoke-filled room
- it may be getting late
- it's often at the cigar and after-dinner drinks stage
- you may be one of three or four speakers
- the audience probably just wants to be entertained
- the audience may be rowdy but highly receptive; it is probably ready to laugh, but equally ready to be distracted and very ready to criticise
- many people will not hear what you say and will need to ask their neighbour
- a number of people won't understand you
- some people won't want to understand you!
- some people will be more preoccupied with how long you are going on for than with what you are actually saying.

Bearing all this in mind, no wonder after-dinner talks are really a topic on their own.

Later we will look at the structure and preparation of your talk. At this stage we are considering the type of presentation you will make. That's the factor that makes after-dinner talks so difficult. You will be standing like a tailor's dummy!

Your words, your delivery, your facial expression – these will be the critical factors.

In several of our presentation situations you may encounter microphones. They can be a blessing or a curse!

Do not spoil your talk if the microphone is incorrectly adjusted. Be patient – wait and insist they get it right.

3　Preparation

From the moment you answer that telephone call, or open the letter asking you to speak, your preparation must begin.

The Venue

Having checked your diary to make sure you are available, it's important immediately to establish a rapport with the organiser. You will find later on that it is most useful to make comprehensive notes at this stage – it will help you in formation of your talk matrix.

　Ask the organiser:

- what is the event entitled?
- where is it to be held?
- at what time does it commence?

- how many speakers will there be?
- what is the topic?
- how long are you expected to speak?
- can he or she let you have directions?
- how many people are expected to attend?
- how big is the room?
- how will it be laid out?
- will there be visual aids available, and if not, is the organiser prepared to hire aids?
- if there are other speakers, what are their topics?
- is it a formal or informal occasion?
- what is the experience and age range of the audience?
- will there be questions?
- is there a fee payable?

In this way you can attempt to get a mental picture of both the event and the venue. You can begin to prepare yourself by picturing yourself there, imagining the audience, deciding upon any visual aids and where they should be placed. It's no use planning electronic visual aids if your talk is to be in an old barn without electric power! But you could use a flip chart . . .

When you decide on your visual aids you must give clear and concise instructions to the organiser. It is best to follow up verbal communications by letter confirming the date, the place, the time and, very important, your visual aid requirements.

Once you arrive, if things are not right, you will find that the organiser will just want you to manage somehow. His or her main concern is that you are there! He or she will expect you to be adaptable; but you know that's not easy when you have already geared up your presentation to a specific routine.

The Talk Notes

In preparing the talk, turn back to your notes from your conversation with the organiser.

Ask yourself:

- what is required of me?

Write down the answer on a large blank piece of paper in big letters.

Now comes the hard part: the brainstorming of the matrix. You must decide on:

- the structure
- the content
- the sequence.

You may immediately get ideas. Scribble them quickly on the same piece of paper. This method will focus your mind. However, your mind may be completely blank!

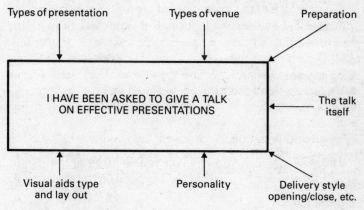

FIGURE 3.1 Talk Matrix

Do what a good surgeon would do when encountering trouble. Don't panic. Return to it later. Unlike the surgeon you're not in a rush. Let it roll over in your mind for a few hours or even a few days.

I must emphasise how really important this first part is. Put down plenty of ideas – you can reduce them later.

Now get down to sequencing the points. Can you work out some sort of logical order?

Most presentations are neatly sequenced into:

- the opening
- the middle
- the end.

Play around with your scribblings.

- Which points will form the main body of your talk?
- Which points would be suitable early on to gain interest in the subject?
- Is there any sort of conclusion?

This process can take hours or seconds! It's totally unpredictable.

Avoid putting things into your talk just because you have used them before. They may be irrelevant. I know it's tempting to cannabalise bits from previous talks; but this is being lazy and your delivery can only be fresh if the material is new.

Let us return to the main types of presentation we discussed in Chapter 2 and see what format of notes will fit in to the different types of presention:

- an in-company presentation
- a talk to a small group
- a training session
- a conference
- an after-dinner talk.

The way in which you develop your matrix, prepare your notes and decide on visual aids will depend on the event itself.

In-company Presentation

We discussed earlier the need for good preparation. If, for example, you were reporting on sales against budget for the Northern Region, most of your colleagues are probably not interested in masses of minute detail about Salespeople X and Y. They are more interested in an *overview*.

Recalling our statement to the meeting: 'I am reporting on sales for the Northern Region. This last quarter we achieved our budgeted sales of £— and in fact I am pleased to report . . .' The supporting document you could be working from could also be used as a hand-out. See Exhibit 3.1.

Company A B C

Annual sales target £_____
Northern Region target £..........(%)

Actuals	First Quarter	Second Quarter	Third Quarter	Fourth Quarter
Area X				
Area Y				
Area Z				
Total actuals				
TARGET £				
VARIANCE ±				

EXHIBIT 3.1

You don't need notes. This hand-out is easy to present from and it also conveys plenty of information at a glance. It tells you the total company sales target and what percentage the Northern Region need to obtain. It gives you the first quarter actuals split into areas and also shows the variance above/below target.

Within your reserve file of information you could have prepared an analysis of sales by salespeople and subdivision to monthly statistics as well.

Sales analysis by area

Month ended:

Area	Sales value £
TOTAL SALES	

EXHIBIT 3.2

Sales analysis by salesman	
Month ended:	
Sales people	Sales value £
TOTAL SALES	

EXHIBIT 3.3

Any tricky questions can be handled from your reserve file if necessary!

Alternatively you could present key figures very effectively

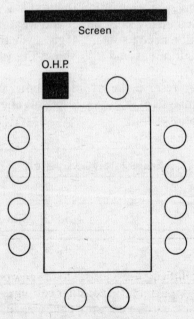

FIGURE 3.2 Room Lay-out showing Overhead Projector

on a flip chart. This again is easy to talk from and at least it introduces a bit of *movement*.

An overhead projector is also very effective. You could remain seated if you wish. Press the button, and there you have some key statistics clearly displayed on the screen. Keep the details brief for maximum effect.

If you are talking about a new product X, add weight to your presentation by showing either:

- a short video on the product in action
- some 35 mm slides
- a hand-out, preferably with a picture or artist's impression of the product as well as some narrative. See Exhibit 3.4.

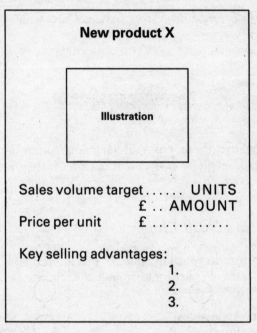

EXHIBIT 3.4

If you find it difficult to do justice to the new product when it is reduced to a small picture, consider cutting out the shape in strong paper or cardboard and enlarging it by using the overhead projector and screen.

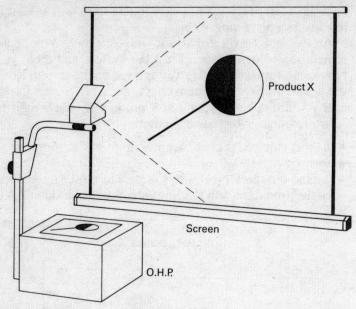

FIGURE 3.3 Displaying illustration of the product

If you use these types of technique, your in-company presentation will be *easy to deliver*, *effectively presented and well received*.

A Talk to a Small Group

Again return to your talk matrix. You are probably trying to give a 'relaxed' performance and this can be achieved by using:

- outline-style notes
- visual aids
- hand-outs.

Remember our first case history? My note preparation was too detailed, as I discovered during the presentation. All you really need is an outline with prompts to keep you on course.

Some speakers prefer the type of notes shown in Exhibit 3.5.

I WANT TO

BEGIN WITH

TECHNICAL DETAILS

OF PRODUCT Z.

Show Slide 1.

EXHIBIT 3.5

The idea is to force you to talk in your own words, introducing the technical details of the product. Then you have the slide prompt which will enable the group to gain a visual impression. This will not only generate interest, but divert the attention away from you towards the screen.

Exhibit 3.6 is an alternative note lay-out, again in outline.

Both methods of notes are far better than having masses of typescript!

EXHIBIT 3.6

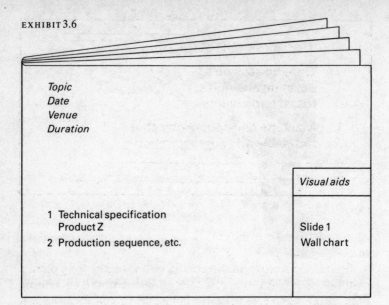

Topic
Date
Venue
Duration

Visual aids

1 Technical specification
  Product Z
2 Production sequence, etc.

Slide 1
Wall chart

If you need to put over a lot of technical data and figures then you are best to have this typed in advance as a hand-out.

Give it out and talk the group through it line by line, or ask them to read it for five minutes and then you can discuss it.

Questions are best dealt with as you go along. This will promote more of an informal atmosphere than a 'straight' presentation by you.

A Training Session

We will now consider the contrasting situations of the course director's preparation and the guest lecturer's (or group leader's) preparation.

The course director must give an effective welcome to the participants and endeavour to establish an early rapport between the group and himself or herself.

The course director's note preparation should be restricted and amount to no more than three or four key documents.

Exhibit 3.7 is an example of a *lead document*. This lead

EXHIBIT 3.7

document gives little more than the essential headings and it's really all you need.

Supporting documentation could be a group seating plan, a course timetable and a course feedback form. The seating plan (see Figure 3.4) will also be useful to enable any guest lecturers to learn the names of participants.

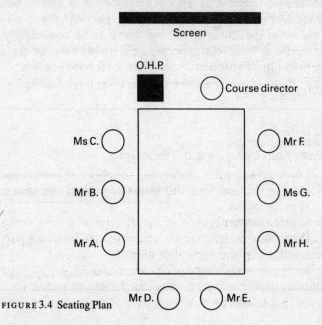

FIGURE 3.4 Seating Plan

Day	a.m. Subject	p.m. Subject
Mon.		
Tues.		
Wed.		
Thurs.		
Fri.		
Sat.		
Sun.		

EXHIBIT 3.8: Course Timetable

You can use the course timetable to talk from during your opening address. Also give it out as a hand-out and go through the timetable with the group. This will help put you and the participants at ease. At the same time you can mention guest lecturers and other events.

The final document is an optional one – a course/talk feedback form. Here you are asking the participants to give their views on specific subjects and 'score' them accordingly. Often feedback forms can generate a discussion base for use in an open-forum situation at the end of the training session.

What, then, of preparation by the lecturer or group leader?

COURSE:

Please help by scoring the following:

	Relevant	Not relevant
1. Course content		
2. Duration		
3.		
4.		

EXHIBIT 3.9: Feedback Form

To a certain extent this is an 'extension' of the situation you encountered in giving a talk to a small group.

The main difference is one of *time*.

- Your presentation to a small group could be twenty minutes to one hour.
- But as a *lecturer* you could be covering a session of between one hour and one day, or even more!

Let us return to the brainstorming matrix described earlier in the chapter. Consider the time factors. Subdivide your talk outline into sections of, say, half-hours (if your presentation is to be of some duration). Then try to build in suitable visual aid options and hand-outs to generate some variety within the time given.

Another useful idea is to prepare some exercises for the participants to work on individually or collectively in small syndicates.

When you are satisfied, put together an overall plan in note form as shown in Exhibit 3.10.

EXHIBIT 3.10

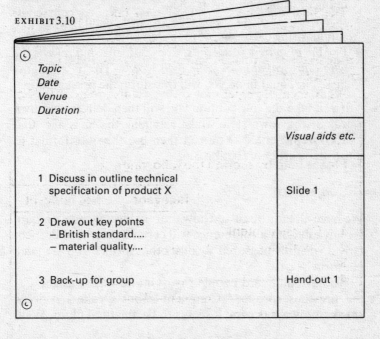

	Visual aids etc.
Topic Date Venue Duration	
1 Discuss in outline technical specification of product X	Slide 1

2 Draw out key points
  – British standard....
  – material quality....	

3 Back-up for group	Hand-out 1

As a guest lecturer, quite frequently you will encounter session notes that have already been prepared containing information that it has been deemed necessary by the course organisers to put over. Here is an example: 'Tell the group the technical specifications of Product Z. Ask them the question: what are the product's main advantages?'

How can you present the information effectively? The problem here is that you are presenting someone else's thoughts and words. If you keep straight to the script, you will definitely be boring!

Of course it is helpful that exercises, hand-outs, etc., have been prepared and we can use them to our advantage. What I am getting at is the difficulty for you, for the presentation can become terribly stiff.

There are three ways in which you can try to overcome this and give a really effective presentation using information already prepared.

- *Highlight key phrases within the notes*, either by under-lining or using a highlighter pen.
- *Insert your own A4 sheets with key words* and information summarising each page of prepared notes.
- *Use the prepared visual aids, exercises, etc., but rewrite the whole presentation in your own words*. This is a lengthy task; but I guarantee you will transform the presentation!

If you take the third option you will then deliver your own words in your own style whilst retaining the 'message' that had to be presented. You can then use the note format as illustrated earlier in Exhibit 3.6.

A Conference

We have already discussed how thoroughly you must prepare for any talk, but a conference will certainly test you! Particularly if you are 'measured' against other speakers on the same platform.

We have all heard people say, 'Oh, he wasn't as good as the previous speaker.' Comment *about* speakers *between* speakers always occurs; it seems to be a natural fill-in. Well, you may not be the best orator on the platform, but with good preparation you can definitely come up with the most *effective presentation*.

Your conference notes and the development of them will evolve from your perception of the venue, the type of conference and the theme. Speakers' presentations vary enormously from reading out a conference paper to extemporising using virtually no notes whatsoever! This latter method will hold the audience's attention better but can only be achieved if there is *great familiarity with the topic*. If not, it's dangerous to try and calls on a lot of courage to talk your way through. Also, timing is much more difficult – you can easily overrun.

Preparing a Conference Paper

If this *must* be done, then try to keep it short. If you can memorise some sections, all the better. You certainly are in danger of boring the pants off everyone by just reading out your paper.

Have your notes typed out in *capital* letters using double spacing. Then mark up words that you wish to emphasise – either underline or use a highlighter pen.

Preparing a 35 mm Slide Projector Presentation

Details of how to operate this are given in Chapter 4. As regards notes you will probably require very few. By using a

EXHIBIT 3.11

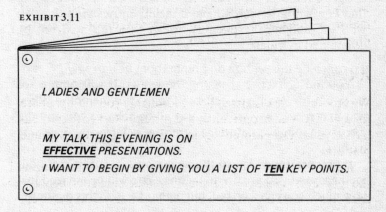

31

rapid sequencing of slides most of the time you will be referring to the screen itself. You will find little attention focused on you and the audience will be concentrating on the screen, particularly if your slide presentation has rapid sequences telling the full story on the screen rather than just highlighting main points as you would tend to do using an overhead projector.

This type of presentation calls for extensive preparation of 35 mm slides. To have this done professionally will prove expensive.

- Aim for variety by interspersing pictures as opposed to all words.
- Try putting two slides together to generate a picture with a caption.
- Try creating negatives which show white lettering on a black background.

Video

This presentation will certainly break up the monotony as there's nothing like a TV screen to hold attention! If there is a large audience, use two TV monitors and get them *elevated* to make sure people can see. Alternatively you can use a 'big-screen' video presentation. Either way, it's a powerful aid to an effective presentation.

As a rough guide, the video should not last for more than about 20 minutes, otherwise it will *detract* from your talk in that you will afterwards have difficulty in *regaining rapport* with the audience! You must use it as a tool and not be dominated by video.

To conclude this section on preparation, *be thorough!*

You must practise speaking the words. It will simply not work out for you if you just run things over mentally. When you first *speak* the words, it may all be alien to you and the words can sound unnatural. Therefore, *stand up and speak the words*.

If you are travelling to the venue by car, speak them out loud again as you are driving along. You will be amazed just how much you can iron out and memorise with this method.

PART II

4   Visual Aids

The information following is by no means exhaustive and is by way of introduction to the most usual types of aid. There is no substitute for experience with different visual aids and you must try to experiment to find the best method to fit in with your particular presentation.

Overhead Projectors

The overhead projector is possibly the best known and most widely used visual aid.

Overhead projectors come in a range of sizes and qualities,

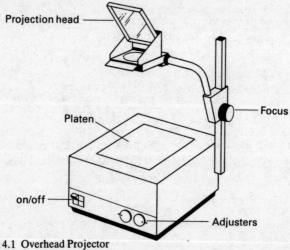

FIGURE 4.1 Overhead Projector

from the 'standard' type of machine covering all the necessary qualities of a 'limited budget' user's requirements through to the 'executive' portable type of machine which comes complete with carrying case.

The lower-cost budget machine will have the following features:

A4 square platen
3-element lens
optical tuning
external colour fringe eliminator
universal retractable locating pins
mains lead storage
super-quiet tangential fan
300-hour lamp (24 V, 250 W)
optional acetate roll facility
positive focusing
cut-out safety switches.

The 'super' type incorporates all these features plus many more options and at the top of the range the 'executive' combines all these features plus:

a choice of A4 or A5 platen area
3-element projection lens
external lamp change mechanism
spring-loaded collapsible projection post
light weight (approximately 11 kg)
revolving head (landscape/portrait use)
lightweight polyurethane body
2 × 300-hour lamps (24 V, 250 W)
carrying case
light output exceeding 2,000 lumen.

Having examined the specification of the projectors, we will consider material (software) preparation and storage.

Software Preparation

There are two main types: *instant* software and *prepared* software.

Instant Software   During discussions and to answer questions raised during talks, the simplest way is to produce material while the audience is watching. To produce instant software the only requirements are clear film (available in sheet or roll form) and felt-tipped overheard projector markers for thick lines, or fibre-tipped OHP markers for thin lines. These markers are readily available in a wide range of colours from your audio-visual supplier. Answers and talking points can thus be reinforced by writing 'on to' the screen as discussion takes place. This method is not only simple but very effective as a means of communication.

Prepared Software   You should remember that when you are preparing software there are a few basic rules.

- *Anything* you can produce on paper can be copied on to your OHP film; the only limitations are your drawing or writing skill and your time. If you have plenty of advance warning, your handiwork can be an excellent accompaniment to your talk. It can also be re-used indefinitely if stored well.
- Don't make drawings or lettering too fine. *Use bold letter-*

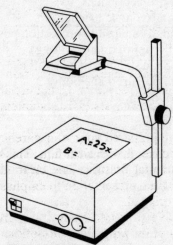

FIGURE 4.2 Preparing Instant Software

ing. Remember what you produce must be totally legible and clear when viewed from the most distant occupied seat. For lettering, work on a safe upper limit of thirty characters per line including spaces. Letters can be hand-written, traced, stencilled or applied ready-made (for example, Letraset). A good rule to follow is to use lower-case letters which are easier to read than capitals of the same size. Also, except for special effects, use or imitate type face.

- Adding colour. Once you have established the size and basic information to be presented on your transparency you may then want to colour it. There are various methods for colouring. For basic colouring you can use felt or fibre OHP markers, or for bar charts, etc. adhesive strip in various colour choices is available. For larger areas, coloured transparent sheets are available. To use the coloured sheeting, simply cut an area slightly larger than the required finished size using a studio knife; pick up a corner of the shape with the knife corner and peel it off, then lay it on the slide you want to colour and trim it to size. Some firms (for example, Letravision) also produce transparent arrows, squares and other symbols; ready-made histograms, comprising parallel strips of colour which need only to be cut to the right length; pie chart sheets and conventional chart sheets; fine and medium spirit markers; correcting markers and trimming knives.

As a variation, a useful purchase for school and college lecturers, etc. is a wide range of prepared transparencies, such as maps and biological subjects. Commercial transparencies are also available showing standard statement, invoice, wage slip, ledger forms, etc.

Once you have prepared your transparency from basic or prepared sheet, cover it with clear film. This protects it from damage or accidental erasure. The clear film can also be written on during the presentation to emphasise points without spoiling the original.

When you have prepared your transparency there are several methods of showing the information. You can either display it all at once or else you can *reveal it line by line*. This is achieved by covering part of the transparency with a card and once the machine is switched on moving the card to reveal one line or one area at a time. To reveal area by area, cut pieces of card and number them, then as talk goes on remove card in the sequence required to reveal the required areas.

Overlaying is possibly one of the most effective visual techniques using transparencies and is achieved by overlaying transparencies with other transparencies. Then the completed print-out can be transferred using your photocopier to a transparency sheet for use on the OHP.

Photocopy prepared transparencies To produce your transparency, simply load the photocopier feed tray with the special transparent sheet and place the material to be copied on the glass of the photocopier. Anything you don't want to reproduce can be masked with white paper. Once your transparency is prepared, colour can be added as required. This method is ideal for the preparation of detailed maps, computer-produced data and any other complex material.

Thermal copiers use a special kind of film and have the limitation that the original to be copied must have a heat-absorbing image. This means that pencil and most black inks will produce good copies but colours may produce only weak copies or may not copy at all! One unique feature of the thermal copier is that it has the ability to convert (using a special film) an original to its negative form. Again, once your transparency is produced, colour can be added as before.

Starter kits Many audio-visual suppliers provide excellent starter kits. These come in various shapes and forms. However, a typical starter kit comprises:

> Sheets of clear and coloured film
> Copier film (specify wet or dry)
> A lay-out board for holding film in register with an alignment grid
> Sheets of dry-transfer lettering and numbers, ready-coloured background transparent sheets, pre-coloured and printed pie charts, and many other self-adhesive symbols and backgrounds.

FIGURE 4.3 Preparing a Bar Chart Transparency

If you have access to a photocopier you can save considerable time and effort by simply transferring your text on to OHP sheets.

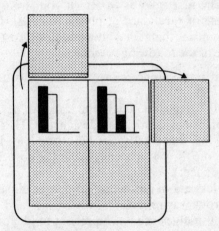

FIGURE 4.4 Overlaying Transparency

There are two special types of transparent sheeting available: one for dry copiers, that is, ones which use powder, and one for liquid copiers. Basically, however, the procedure is identical.

Computer prepared OHP slides. If you have access to a computer graphics program then this can be used to produce bar charts, pie charts, etc. See Figure 4.5.

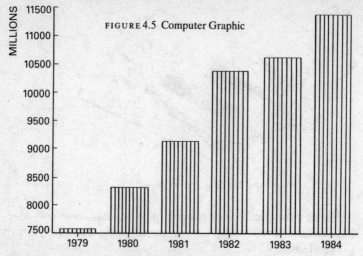

FIGURE 4.5 Computer Graphic

Storage The first stage is to attach your transparencies to frames made of cardboard or plastic material. I'm sure you will find mounting them for a little additional cost essential for at least one of the following reasons:

- Mounted transparencies are less likely to become damaged.
- If the OHP has a hot platen, the transparency will not curl and spoil focus (with well-designed OHPs and good-quality films this should not be a problem, but if this is encountered the transparency should be covered with glass or acrylic sheet).
- There is less risk of projecting a mounted film upside-down or the wrong way round.
- There is usually space on the mount to identify the transparency and make a few notes or statistics.
- A mounted transparency can be located on the OHP platen more accurately, especially if the platen has locating pins.
- Mounted transparencies are much easier to handle than loose transparencies.

Mounted transparencies can then be filed in folders. See Figure 4.6.

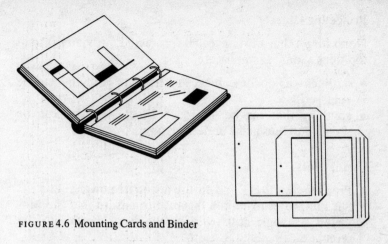

FIGURE 4.6 Mounting Cards and Binder

A patented binder system for transparencies is now on the market. This enables transparencies to be projected without removing them from the binder. To use this system:

Attach self-adhesive strip to the edge of the transparency and then fix strip into wire binding.
You may bind in your notes relevant to each transparency opposite to it.
Attach binder to projector
    (see Figure 4.7).
Project.

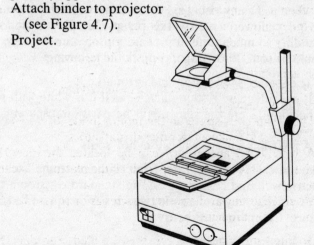

FIGURE 4.7 Binder on Overhead Projector

Projecting Objects

Don't forget that any item can be projected, providing it's not too thick. Some examples are:

- outlines – an opaque object such as a leaf or feather can be enlarged.
- anything that can be improved by enlargement can be shown and thus assist understanding.

Useful Hints

- Prepare your OHP and ensure adequate power points.
- Set the projector screen distance to ensure that the projected rectangle just overlaps the black border of the screen.
- Ensure that you have all transparencies to hand with spare lamp, pens and spare sheets *before* the audience arrives.
- Test clarity with first slide by viewing yourself from the back of the room.

The Screen

No matter how good your transparencies are and your OHP is, when using any visual aid the screen is of vital importance. An old, yellowed screen will simply spoil the picture, and after spending so much time in preparation of your software this would be soul-destroying. So check the following:

- The screen is not yellow and age marked.
- It has adequate backing layers, as if it is white with poor backing layers the screen will be partly transparent and will lose light.
- A too shiny surface will cause 'hot' spots.

Like the OHP, screens vary from economy to the exclusive electric wall and ceiling type. The standard classroom type screen is generally available in two sizes, 50 in square and 60 in square. Common features are:

Vinyl and steel case
Fibreglass tear-proof material

Wall or ceiling mounting
Flame and mildew resistance
Fabric to roller adhesive quality
Steel bottom edged
Integral end cap/mounting brackets
Double stitched bottom edged.

A superior quality screen is availabe for lectures or conferences 70 in square or 96 in square. There are giant screens for large lecture rooms and auditoriums and these can be 10 ft square or 12 ft square.

Possibly the most popular type to go with the portable OHP projector are the tripod-mounted screens. These come in various sizes again ranging from 50 in square (ideal for small conference rooms) to 96 in square. The main features of these screens are:

walnut, vinyl or chrome finish
built-in keystone eliminator
fabric-lock roller preventing fabric separation
fully lockable leg system
adjustable case height
legs with plastic tips
anchor handle
flame and mildew resistance.

The electric screen is available currently in four main sizes 70 in square, 8 ft, 10 ft or 12 ft square. It's a matter of choice. Basically the screens incorporate all the usual features together with an electrically operated mechanism:

3-position switches
anti-vibration rubber mounting
thermal overload protection
automatic stop in up or down mode
electric braking in any position
integral end cap
wall or ceiling brackets
fire and mildew resistance.

An extremely popular 'on the road' model is the dual-legged portable front or rear projection screen. These screens are available in a carrying case; they have aluminium frames and generally can be set up without tools. They are available by special order to your audio-visual supplier in five sizes from 5 ft to 12 ft.

Projectors

35 mm slide projectors come in a range of sizes and prices starting at the very basic filmstrip/slide projector through the range to the exclusive Ringmaster-type carousel projector complete with its own screen, remote control and sound system.

Filmstrip/slide Projector

An example of the simplest type of filmstrip/slide projector would normally be described as having the following features:

> low-voltage lamp
> efficient cooling system
> drop-in interchangeable filmstrip and slide carrier
> high-performance lens
> tilt adjustment
> glass carrier for keeping transparencies flat
> integral carrying handle
> selection of lenses.

Basically filmstrip/slide projectors are a useful visual aid when showing a small selection of slides or film as an aid to your talk.

If, however, continuity in the slide sequence is of greater importance or you require a more professional slide show, perhaps you may wish to utilise one of the range of carousel type projectors available on the market today.

Carousel Projectors

The Kodak carousel projector   This is a 35 mm slide projector with a rotary slide holder (carousel). The basic S A V 1030 projector would normally have the following features:

single solo projection
adjustable elevation
one-second slide change
manual or remote focus control
low-voltage lamps
universal lens mount to accept lenses with even length focal lengths
adaptable condenser system for 35 mm slides/super-slides and/or longer focal length lenses.

At the top of the carousel projector range is the SAV 2050. It has all the features of the solo projector but with additional features, including:

dissolve (multiple) projection
built-in solenoid operated 'snap change' shutter, controllable via an external 12-pin socket
An LED light, which indicates when slide tray is in zero position.

The Ringmaster projector   This incorporates all the carousel benefits plus having an audio-visual facility through a TV screen monitor and is the top of the carousel range. There are currently three models available on the market which allows you to select the most cost-effective type of unit to meet your communication needs most effectively. These high performance projectors offer you a range from a simple playback unit to a multi-function, microprocessor-controlled, programmable record/edit/playback model. As these are a modern and up-to-date method of releasing you from the limitations of sequential slide display, I will explore their features in some detail.

The professional slide/pulsed tape presenter   The Ringmaster RM820 has many advantages over the standard carousel projector. With its built-in monitor screen it can be extremely useful when addressing a small audience. However, by a simple adjustment it can be changed over to project on to a large screen (as used for OHP).

The machine has a shift mechanism which silently transfers

the slides while the screen remains black. The mechanism can be operated manually or can be used for automatic slide transfer at a minimum 1.5-second change if required.

An automatic focus system is incorporated; therefore, as soon as the first slide is focused manually, the automatic focus system takes over. This allows you to utilise a variety of different slide thicknesses during your programme.

The machine has a built-in speaker and the volume/tone control can be adjusted to match the auditorium size and output. An external speaker can also be connected for larger audiences. An optional microphone is also available.

In some locations it is not always necessary to use the full light output and a 'Hi' 'Lo' lamp setting which reduces the voltage input to the lamp is incorporated. This gives a slight reduction in brightness and has also been found to give a substantial increase in average lamp life.

In the base of the machine there is a useful storage compartment which can be used for storing your slide tray and cassettes.

Combined production/presenter and training unit The RM 840 can be used with a network of RM 820 machines or individually. In industry and colleges in particular the RM 840 is very useful in that it can be used as a learning laboratory. The machine can be fitted with a headphones lead and by using the cue-stop feature the user can follow the demonstration and also participate at his or her own pace.

The programme production is simple. First, you get your script together, then prepare the slides, record the commentary and record the advance cue stops and pulse required. The programmes you record on this machine comply with the International Pulsing standards (1,000 hz) and thus will play with accurate synchronisation on any other machine which complies with the standard.

The machine has an operational remote control accessory, so the live presenter can take complete control manually if required and can forward or reverse slide movements or freeze the programme at a particular point, or restart the projector after a cue stop.

Programmable sound/slide system   The deluxe model RM 850 in this range combines all the features of the previous two models, but it has further extras.

It can present any slides, in any sequence and with a synchronised sound system.

It has a random access response to keyboard command, thus allowing a particular slide to be selected by remote control.

Continuous advance is available automatically at pre-set intervals.

It has a pause and advance feature which can be automatically programmed.

There is an instant digital slide identification.

As with the RM 840 an optional infra-red remote control is available.

How can these features assist you in your presentation?

With the keyboard command you can easily call any slide to the screen by simply dialling in its number. Three-digit numbers are generally used to give the machine its commands.

To enable you to keep in touch with the position you are in in your programme, the slide number is shown on the display simultaneously as it appears on the screen.

The built-in timer has three settings – 5 seconds, 10 seconds and 15 seconds depending on the speed of slide presentation you require. Of course by using the optional remote control, at up to a distance of 10 metres from the projector, the keyboard command can be overriden at your request. The built-in timer can also be used for 'unattended' presentations. This is particularly useful in the direct 'point of sale' type of presentation.

The system has a 'binary coded pulses' feature which allows you to identify each of the 80 or 140 slots on the tray. Because of this your programme can again be adjusted to the type of situation, by showing either part or the whole of your programme, or repeating sections of the programme. You need to find the selected place on the cassette and the tray will automatically rotate to the correct slide.

By recording another tape with all the required new slide pulses and new commentary, you can change to a complete new slant on the presentation without having to change the slides, or their positions, on the tray. An example: you have a set of slides showing the manufacture of a car from basic principles to the finished production. You could produce two tapes using the same slides, one tape as a 'sales demonstration presentation' and by simply changing the tape turn the presentation into a 'training programme' presentation.

Slide Storage

In the Ringmaster type there is a compartment for storing a number of slides, which is ideal for storing during transit. But where many slides are used, storage is very important.

Storage can be made in simple indexed slide boxes or in a range of slide storage cabinets. One of the popular type of slide storage cabinets comprises a built-in light box with a dust resistant cabinet with either vertical or horizontal viewing. Fifty-four slides are mounted in each tray and capacity ranges from 10 trays (540 slides) to 80 trays (4,320 slides).

Another type of slide storage cabinet is the System 4000 series available from your audio-visual supplier. Its features are as follows:

- It accommodates three different slide sizes: 2×2 in, $4 \times 3\frac{1}{4}$ in, and $2\frac{3}{4} \times 2\frac{3}{4}$ in, as well as 4×5 in transparencies, which can be filed in special plastic protective sleeves. Capacity varies obviously by cabinet size, but an example of holding frames is 120 each 2×2 in, 36 each $4 \times 3\frac{1}{4}$ in, 63 each $2\frac{3}{4} \times 2\frac{3}{4}$ in and 25 4×5 in transparencies. The example cabinet holds 33 frames, and frames of all four types can be mixed in the same cabinet.

- Cross-indexing and recording of slides is achieved by numbering each slide within the corresponding frame, then entering them with contents reference on index sheet. For example, on Tray 3 slide number 16, subject: house demolition, would be indexed as '3:16–house demolition' on the reference register.

- Trays pull out for *in situ* viewing and updating of slides. Slides are mounted between plastic channels and slide out for changing. Integral light box is available.

- Cabinets are available with duplicate slide storage facility. Again slides can be numerically indexed to correspond with the slides in frame.

- Cabinets can be desk mounted, or be mounted on duplicate slide storage cabinet or mounted on 'T' bases, stationary or on castors.

The Flip Chart

The flip chart is basically a pad of paper with information written on it. Generally it is mounted on an easel and as the talk proceeds it can be flipped over to the next piece of information.

Flip chart easels are generally lightweight portable items and the pads can be purchased to suit. Some easels are freestanding or they can be desk mounted. Special pens are used for flip charts and flip pads. These are dry-wipe or wet-wipe pens and can be purchased in a variety of colours.

A fairly recent innovation on the market is a Conference Cabinet. This comprises a lockable cabinet which can be wall mounted or supplied with its own mobile base. The cabinet contains two flip pads, one on either door, with a central colour-board. The doors each have a shelf which comes complete with a set of dry-wipe markers and coloured magnetic discs.

Another idea is to use a dual presenter. The dual presenter has a two-part steel frame with a double-sided dry-wipe

Infoboard and two Al flip pad clamps. The Infoboard has a metal dry-wipe surface that can be used for writing on, or for displaying self-adhesive or magnetic accessories, or even for using with an OHP. In the frame the Infoboard is reversible, so the flip pads can be mounted on one side and turned as required.

Whiteboards

These come generally in several finishes, from the lightweight magnetic whiteboard to the deluxe porcelain enamel magnetic whiteboard.

Generally all whiteboards have dry-wipe surfaces and strong metal backs, often pre-drilled for wall mounting. These can be used with a range of magnetic accessories as well as standard self-adhesive symbols. Pens for whiteboards come in a variety of colours and can be various thicknesses dependent on the finishing detail you wish to achieve. The pens are available for dry-wipe or wet-wipe applications. The more favoured for audience presentation is the dry-wipe type.

Good-quality whiteboards can also be used as OHP projection screens, ideal if one or more presenters wish to use a variety of techniques at the same presentation.

Showboards

For the larger type of exhibition where information is to be displayed on a more permanent basis these free-standing display boards come into use. Showboard applications include conferences, product launches, seminars, in-store and window display, exhibitions, demonstrations and presentations.

Panels start at 1 ft wide × 1 ft deep to 6 ft deep × 4 ft wide and fit into poles with snap fit fixing clips. Panels are generally covered with Nyloop fabric, and are double-sided.

Varying panel sizes can be used to give interesting configurations and the angle of the panels can be adjusted to give the desired shape.

Kits are also available from some suppliers, ranging from a basic noticeboard to an extremely elaborate product-launch type of kit.

The foldaway type of showboard system is, as its name suggests, a linked system of showboards which fold away into a flat pack. The foldaway has a total display area of 36 sq. ft made up from six 3 ft × 2 ft panels linked together with hinges. Accessories are available which includes literature holders in perspex, clamp on spotlights with 75 W bulbs, nylon transport bags, a 2 ft × 6 in header board and four-way plug sockets.

Generally these are an excellent system for those stationary 'walk around' displays.

Electrosonic Units

This system is intended for synchronising two and three projector shows. Generally of a heavy duty construction, the unit is suitable for fixed installation, continuous running or 'on the road' travelling.

A back-up audio system has a heavy-duty logic-controlled tape deck with minimum audio controls, volume, treble, bass and noise reduction control. Output of the high-quality stereo sound system is in excess of 20 W rms per channel. An internal monitor loudspeaker is incorporated which disconnects automatically when the extension loudspeakers are connected.

When showing information with a more serious content a two projector system is preferable and a timer FM mode gives continuous dissolving between the two projectors. With the three projector mode you have the full sophistication of multi-image computer controlled shows.

On the show mode control switch there are four basic settings:

- *Line up* – this puts on the projector lamps for alignment.
- *Presentation* – all tape deck functions are operator controlled on this setting.
- *Continuous* – at the end of each showing the projectors reset to zero and the tape rewinds and the show restarts.
- *Autopresent* – the programme is started by pressing the

remote 'start' button. Once the show has run through, the tape resets, the projector goes back to ZERO and the projector is switched off automatically. An auxiliary socket gives control of the 'house lights' provided a suitable dimmer is already installed.

Multi-image Electrosonic Unit

This is the ultimate multi-image machine which is capable of using one or more 'stacks' of three projectors, that is, three to a maximum of twenty-four projectors can be linked in.

The heart of the machine is the tape deck which has a heavy-duty three-motor mechanism with logic control. This combination gives electronic deck function control, electronic tape counter, an eject mechanism for the cassettes which is solenoid operated, and the C60 tape rewinds in 35 seconds with controlled deceleration to prevent tape breaks.

Alphasync   The unit contains a computer tape interface. In the record mode this receives signals from a computer source and converts them into Alphasync signal to be recorded on to the magnetic tape. In the replay mode, the method is reversed and the signal is decoded back and distributed to one or more (up to a maximum of eight) projector interfaces. The Alphasync signal includes slide position information. This means that irrespective of where the tape is started the show will get into sync and also allows for different tapes showing different slide sequences (for example, an English tape showing English graphic slides, a German tape showing German graphic slides, and so on).

Programmes are generally computer produced which allows the full range of effects possible to be utilised on up to twenty-four projectors.

Presentation of the show is in three ways, as on the simpler, maximum of three projector unit – either presentation, continuous or autopresent.

Accessories available are a carrying case, compact high-fidelity speakers with cable, and portable loudspeakers. Again, an auxiliary control is available for house lights, motorised curtains, etc.

Video

In addition to using video in a student training session by filming participants, video is also an extremely popular presentation system. The choice is yours. You can either make your own video using a video camera, with or without sound recording facility, or you can get a video made for you. There are many companies who specialise in making professional videos for corporate businesses.

An audio-visual company that produces your video for you will provide as full a service as required from the initial scripting through to the finished product.

Let us examine some of the equipment you would need to make a do-it-yourself type of video.

The Camera

There are various cameras available. Some cameras have basic qualities such as lightweight bodies, with display unit in the viewfinder which keeps the user informed as to battery power, centring, white balancing, etc. A recent innovation on the market is a camera with *built-in* recording facility. This camera weighs just 25 kilos and can shoot continuously for up to 3 hours 35 minutes. Another type of camera recently developed to aid people seeking higher quality in their video recording is a three-tube video camera. These cameras have a number of automated functions together with a range of accessories and options.

Video Recorder

A range of portable recorders are available. Lightweight and compact, these portable recorders offer many special features including line/camera selection which allows programme assembly from two video sources, backspace editing, an automatic switch-off if machine is left on pause for more than 7 minutes, automatic and manual audio recording level control, and selectable two-speed picture search.

Editor, Edit Control and Director Units

To help with your video film finishing, an automatic editor is available which has many features to enable the serious programme maker to give speed precision to editing programmes. Edit control systems aim to assist fast, accurate editing. Features include a high degree of speed control from one-thirtieth to ten times normal speed in forward and reverse, automatic insert and assembly edit functions, return jump facility, complete logic control, time display and autoset start of assembly edit points.

The director unit is aimed at the more professional video maker and comprises a special effects colour generator, universal Chroma keyer and a wide pattern extender. The combination gives a video switcher/special effects generator with input connectors for six colour cameras, one playback VTR, a camera for external keying and a monochrome camera for downstream key operation. A range of outputs are provided for two preset monitors and three programme monitors.

Playback/Record Monitor

A machine is available which allows recording or playback of stereo or bi-lingual programmes, dubbing facilities, fast and fine still picture search and facility, automatic long pause, auto rewind and logic control.

Video Image Creation

A micro-computer linked with a video interface and superimpose facility allows live or recorded video signals to be combined and synchronised with graphs, graphics and computer data.

The graphics facility is capable of producing a wide range of graphics in up to sixteen colours. An optional extra available is a light pen which can be used for drawing graphics direct on to the screen.

Editing control allows the computer effects to be pre-listed in sequence and then programmed to appear exactly when required, either as standard text, superimposed or mixed images.

The image detail produced by these machines is ideally suited to programmes with high business graphics content which is intended for large screen exposure.

Video Projector

We will look in more detail at the video projector later, but basically the video projector is a compact, generally lightweight unit which projects high resolution pictures from any signal source.

The projectors are designed for desk top, ceiling or floor mounting and are generally simple to use, allowing one person to transport, set up and use the unit.

Portable Video/Display Unit

Another recent innovation in the audio-visual aid market is a combined VHS recorder with miniature monitor screen available in a single carrying case. The unit comes complete with record/replay machine, has approximate dimensions of $22 \times 17 \times 10$ in and weighs approximately 14 kg.

These machines can be operated with a camera and for larger audiences can be connected to a larger monitor. The unit can be used with the mains supply or be battery operated.

16 mm Projectors

16 mm projectors have been available for almost sixty years and are still an extremely popular form of audio-visual aid. The projectors are being constantly updated to anticipate users' changing needs.

In some 16 mm projector applications, the basic requirement is that the machine produces good-quality pictures and sound. Other users may require more functions, such as a means of recording sound or of 'freezing' a single frame of the film on the screen, the latter feature being of particular importance in education and training situations.

The picture quality depends upon the optical system, precise alignment and the lens. The film in a 16 mm projector has to be advanced, halted and advanced again twenty-four times in every second, thus the necessary accuracy must be engineered into the machine's film advancement mechanism. Durability of components is equally important, as in an hour programme the machine goes through the start-stop sequence no fewer than 86,400 times.

Brightness of picture is also of great importance and this is dependent on the efficiency of the lens. The aperture of the lens in most up-to-date machines is f 1.2. An efficient lamp source is also of infinite importance.

To ensure good sound, most projectors have a heavy, dynamically balanced flywheel with an effective stabiliser system which combines to prevent 'wow and flutter'. Projectors generally have one built-in speaker and can have external speakers connected to them.

Because 16 mm film is exceptionally delicate, is expensive to replace and is sometimes used by inexperienced users, film projection is of great importance. Projection of the film begins at the threading in of the film. Automatic threading is an asset introduced into certain projectors. With the automatic threading system one mistake can be made. If this happens, the film automatically escapes from the system, thus protecting the film and then you start again. However, if you require only to show the beginning of the film on the spool, you would have to unthread the rest of the film manually with the automatic threading system, a time-consuming and possibly damaging operation. Therefore a new system has been incorporated into some models in which it is only necessary to press a lever and withdraw the film, in one continuous movement, from the threading slot. Threading at any intermediate point in the film is just as simple to achieve.

Magnetic recording on to a thin strip which is affixed to the edge of the film also features on some projectors. This enables good-quality, exactly synchronised sound to be produced. This also allows for conversion of a conventionally recorded commentary to a different language, for example.

Other projectors have now been produced with exceptionally high-intensity discharge lamps, which are extremely useful in presentations where the auditorium is very large or on exhibition stands when the picture has to compete with 'in-house lighting'.

In a large auditorium when the machine may be a long way from the screen and the presenter, remote control facilities for the main functions are now available for distances of up to 75 m. For non-stop showing of feature length films, by connecting two projectors with an accessory cable link, built-in circuits in the machines can, by push button control, achieve automatic change-overs. Projects can also be adapted for synchronisation of films with slides and other displays.

All 16 mm projectors are supported by a comprehensive range of accessories, including alternative lenses (anamorphic and zoom), screens, stands, speakers, trolleys, microphones, etc.

Large Screen Video Projection

This system provides the versatility of a video system with the impact of a big screen presentation. These machines can be used without using parabolic screens and without the need for special installation.

Features of the large screen video projector include:

- high light output – high resolution lenses.
- 1.50–3.40 m diagonal, flat and curved screens as standard – larger screen sizes possible with optional lens set.
- an optional plug in calibration circuit allows use of cylindrical and parabolic screens.
- front and rear projection, table operated or ceiling mounted.
- multi-colour systems and data reproduction.

A cable remote control or optional source selector is available. To achieve perfect overlapping of the three colours projected, green, blue and red, machines have a unique conveyance system by which the screen is divided into nine zones, each of which can be adjusted without interaction. The end result is excellent sharpness of picture without any colour deviations.

Connection possibilities to the machine are the video tape recorder, video disc camera, off air tuner, computer graphics terminal or remote control and in fact any combination of the above can be directly linked to the projector or through an optional source selector.

Accessories include source selector, additional receiver, demodulator, projection table, flight case, ceiling mount bracket and optional large screen lenses.

5   Giving the Talk

This is it at last!

You have prepared your notes and visual aids thoroughly and now it's time to get stuck in . . .

The Setting

Try and prepare things as much in advance as you can. By telephone ask and verify

- the type of venue?
- the size of room?
- the expected audience?
- the seating arrangements?

- the points of location of the various visual aids?
- is there a platform?
- is there a spare bulb for the OHP?
- will there be a microphone? (if so what type, table or clip-on?)

The seating arrangements are important. Try to get people close together rather than sitting at the back if it's a large room. Atmosphere will be difficult to generate if you are talking to a dispersed audience group.

When the seating is arranged, I like to have access to the back row if necessary. If I am giving a 'roving' style presentation – I like a centre aisle to enable me to move freely into the audience!

Even with a small group seating is important. Remember my first talk!

Here is the layout I faced – this was shown in Chapter 1.

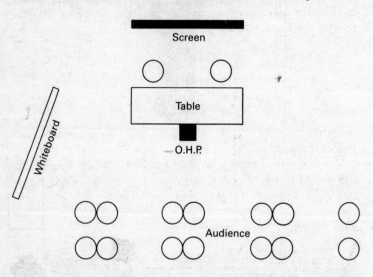

Remember the difficulties I had by not checking the room *before* the audience arrived. The whiteboard and OHP screen were incorrectly positioned. Just a few minutes' work would have given a rearranged situation and made my talk more effective and easier to present.

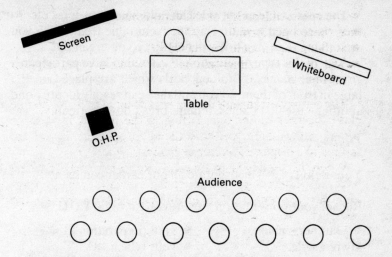

With group training I prefer a 'horse-shoe' shape with centre top table and visual aid facilities that can be used/moved easily at both wings of the table.

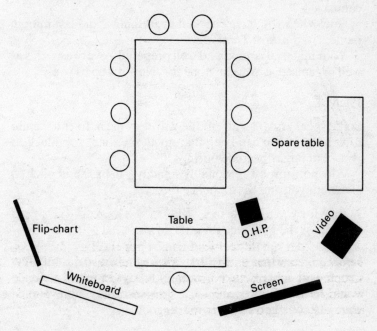

The spare table at the side can hold handouts/notes etc. so there is no need to clutter-up the front table from which you are talking. Keeping tidy will help keep you organised.

Also in this type of situation it's useful to have participants write their names on folded cards which are placed on the table in front of them, so you and they can readily identify one another – use first names; it helps break down formality.

Delivery

Your delivery will incorporate all our earlier comments.

Recap: your presentation must revolve around **YOU**.

- your personality
- your style
- your material
- your preparation
- your rehearsal
- your experience.

Try and arrive early to check the seating arrangements; check the visual aids – give yourself time to 'settle' and be calm.

Now when you have checked everything avoid last minute panic. *Use Positive Thinking*.

Your material is good and well prepared – every aspect is as well organised as you can hope for. Now it's up to you!

Pitch

Some speakers will start off the way they mean to end – quite forcefully. If you can keep that up *all* the time, good luck to you – but it may become boring.

Why not start off reasonably steadily – in pace and pitch to give both you and the audience time . . .

- time for you to settle in
- time for the audience to settle down.

I hold a theory that for the first opening seconds of a talk, few people will actually take in what you say! In my experience they are usually preoccupied by *visual* observation. Hence you must look good and *try* to feel good.

Pace

How quickly you gain momentum seems impossible to predict. Sometimes right from the start – sometimes you may feel 'edgy' all the way through. Also it will depend on the visual aids you are using. Lifting OHP slides on and off takes longer than clicking away during a 35 mm slide presentation.

DO NOT try and fit three hours of material into a one hour presentation!

You might gabble through at rehearsal but there's no chance when you're *live*.

At this point in the book, it's time to include some case-studies for you to examine and place yourself in *the role of the presenter*.

Don't worry too much about the various mathematical calculations, but try to visualise yourself actually presenting in each of the three case-studies.

To maximise the benefits, use my prepared visual aids and have a go!

The case-studies cover:

- a board presentation
- a conference presentation
- a group-leading presentation.

Case-study I – Company A

Scenario

You are the Finance Manager of Company A – manufacturers. Your Board of Directors are keen to receive suggestions from employees, but any suggestions which will affect the Company's financial position are routed through you for financial analysis and for your subsequent presentation to the Board. You have received two suggestions – the first from the Sales team, the second from the Production department.

Your Board is a small team and a professional one. You *must* give a professional and *effective* presentation.

The Presentation

Good morning.

I have been asked to look at two new suggestions received from the Sales and Production departments and, as you know, in my role as Finance Manager I often need to examine profit-orientated suggestions and decide their effect on our company's profitability.

How do I carry out this analysis?

I have started with the basic concept that in our company:

SLIDE 1

SOME OF OUR COMPANY'S COSTS VARY WITH
VOLUME OF PRODUCTION

SOME OF OUR COSTS DO NOT!

Let me explain. Here (*slide 2 on page opposite*) is a list of our costs summarised into areas:

You will see I have separated our costs into those which will *increase proportionately to volume of units produced* and costs which will be the same *irrespective of how many units we make.*

For example, our material content is £3.50 per unit, and our office/admin. costs are 'fixed' at £42,750 per annum.

Costs are known as *variable* (volume-orientated) or *fixed* costs.

Here is an analysis (*pie chart opposite*) of our *variable costs* per unit:

You will note that direct labour is our highest cost at 45.3 per cent per unit manufactured, and materials are second at 35.9 per cent.

Now an analysis of *fixed costs* (*pie chart on page 66*):

This time our major fixed costs are office/admin. costs at 60.8 per cent, with plant and machinery second at 20.0 per cent.

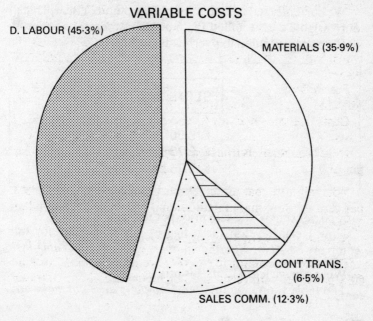

SLIDE 2

Cost per unit of production

materials	£3.50
contract transport	£0.63
sales commission	£1.20
direct labour	£4.42
TOTAL	£9.75

Other costs per annum

office/admin. costs	£42,750
fixed plant and machinery	£14,000
marketing	£ 5,000
other overheads	£ 8,430
TOTAL	£70,180

VARIABLE COSTS

D. LABOUR (45·3%)

MATERIALS (35·9%)

CONT TRANS. (6·5%)

SALES COMM. (12·3%)

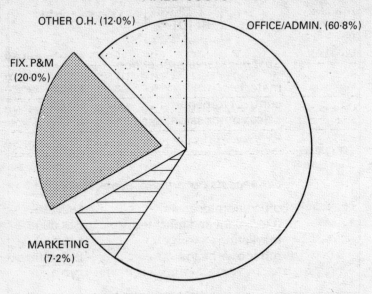

FIXED COSTS

OTHER O.H. (12·0%)
OFFICE/ADMIN. (60·8%)
FIX. P&M (20·0%)
MARKETING (7·2%)

We currently sell our units at £19.50 per unit. You will recall our variable costs totalled £9.75 per unit; therefore our gross profit or contribution to overheads per unit is

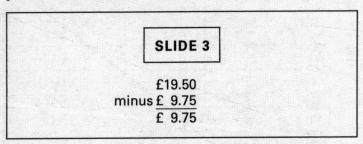

SLIDE 3

£19.50
minus £ 9.75
£ 9.75

– or 50 per cent of the sale price per unit sold.

Now I can develop these figures into a 'profile' for our company *based on differing numbers of units sold* (*Table 1*):

What can we learn from this profile?

The table shows me that *this Company does not make any*

TABLE 1

Fixed costs			£70,000	**Company A profile**		
Variable costs as % sales			50			
Unit sale price			£19.50			

Units sold	0	2,000	4,000	6,000	8,000	10,000
Sales	£0	£39,000	£78,000	£117,000	£156,000	£195,000
Variable costs	£0	£19,500	£39,000	£58,500	£78,000	£97,500
Gross profit	£0	£19,500	£39,000	£58,500	£78,000	£97,500
Fixed costs	£70,000	£70,000	£70,000	£70,000	£70,000	£70,000
Net profit	(£70,000)	(£50,500)	(£31,000)	(£11,500)	£8,000	£27,500
Gross profit %	0%	50%	50%	50%	50%	50%
Total costs	£70,000	£89,500	£109,000	£128,500	£148,000	£167,500

profit until we sell in excess of *6,000 units*. At 8,000 units we should make £8,000 net profit. If we reach sales of 10,000 units, then we make £27,500 profit.

I find it useful to illustrate our company profile graphically by plotting units of production against £ (thousands)

COMPANY 'A' PROFILE
F.C. £70 K – V.C. 50% – PRICE £19·50

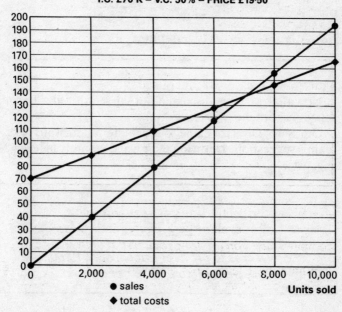

● sales
◆ total costs

Units sold

The graph shows costs commencing at £70,000 (our fixed costs level) and finishing up at £167,500 total costs (which we saw in Table 1), on the basis of 10,000 units sold.

The sales line on the graph commences at zero and ends up at £195,000–10,000 units sold, at £19.50 per unit.

The point at which the total costs line and the sales line cross is the *break-even point*. This is the point where we make *neither* profit nor loss.

From the graph you can see that break-even occurs at £140,000 of sales, or approximately 7,000 units.

Our sales team currently has a planned sales quota of 9,000 units to be sold, and I can therefore be aware that our 'margin of safety' is £35,500 of sales. This is:

SLIDE 4

Planned level of sales (per quota)	£175,500	(9,000 units @ £19.50)
less break-even sales	£140,000	
net	£ 35,500	

or 20%

– this looks a reasonable margin.

Now that we have discussed our current profile, I want to tell you about the first suggestion.

Our Sales Director came to see me to put forward his sales team's suggestion, following their usual monthly meeting. He suggests:

SLIDE 5

Decrease product price from £19.50 per unit to £15.25 per unit.

His team estimate that by decreasing the unit sale price they can increase sales from their 9,000 unit quota to possibly 10,000 units.

A typical sales team suggestion!

Decrease price   *Increase* volume.

What effect will this have on company profitability? Let me recap on unit costs:

<table>
<tr><td colspan="3" align="center">**SLIDE 6**</td></tr>
<tr><td>materials</td><td>£3.50</td><td></td></tr>
<tr><td>contract transport</td><td>£0.63</td><td></td></tr>
<tr><td>sales commission</td><td>£1.20</td><td></td></tr>
<tr><td>direct labour</td><td>£4.42</td><td></td></tr>
<tr><td>TOTAL</td><td>£9.75</td><td>(50% of product sale price)</td></tr>
</table>

Now the sales team's suggestion will not affect any of the costs per unit, except sales commission, which is based on 6.2 per cent of unit sale price:

$$\text{comm.} \quad \frac{£\,1.20}{£19.50} \times 100 = 6.2\%$$
$$\text{price}$$

Reducing the sales price to £15.25, then, the new variable costs per unit become:

<table>
<tr><td colspan="3" align="center">**SLIDE 7**</td></tr>
<tr><td>materials</td><td>£3.50</td><td></td></tr>
<tr><td>cont. transport</td><td>£0.63</td><td></td></tr>
<tr><td>sales commission</td><td>£0.95</td><td>(£15.25 @ 6.2%)</td></tr>
<tr><td>direct labour</td><td>£4.42</td><td></td></tr>
<tr><td>TOTAL</td><td>£9.50</td><td>(62.3% of product sale price)</td></tr>
</table>

Calculating volume sales as before:

Fixed costs			£70,000			
Variable costs as % sales			62.3			
Unit sale price			£15.25			
Units sold	0	2,000	4,000	6,000	8,000	10,000
Sales	£0	£30,500	£61,000	£91,500	£122,000	£152,500
Variable costs	£0	£19,000	£38,000	£57,000	£76,000	£95,000
Gross profit	£0	£11,500	£23,000	£34,500	£46,000	£57,500
Fixed costs	£70,000	£70,000	£70,000	£70,000	£70,000	£70,000
Net profit	(£70,000)	(£58,500)	(£47,000)	(£35,500)	(£24,000)	(£12,500)
Gross profit %	0%	37.7%	37.7%	37.7%	37.7%	37.7%
Total costs	£70,000	£89,000	£108,000	£127,000	£146,000	£165,000

So much for that suggestion!

Even at the new suggested volume of sales of 10,000 units *we do not make a profit*. In fact – a loss of £5,500 would be incurred!

Persevering for just a minute, I will demonstrate this graphically (*graph opposite*).

The gap between total costs and sales is narrowing, but break-even is not reached. Using a formula:

SLIDE 8

$$\text{Break-even sales} = \frac{\text{Fixed costs}}{\text{g.p.\%}}$$

$$\text{then Break-even sales} = \frac{£70,000}{37.7\%}$$

$$= £185,676$$

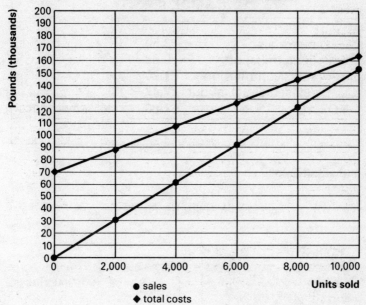

COMPANY 'A' PROFILE
F.C. £70 K – V.C. 57·7% – PRICE £15·25

Pounds (thousands)

200
190
180
170
160
150
140
130
120
110
100
90
80
70
60
50
40
30
20
10
0

0   2,000   4,000   6,000   8,000   10,000

Units sold

● sales
◆ total costs

then you can project that the required *break-even* sales level would be £185,000, based on this suggestion, and at the proposed reduced sale price of £15.25 would require a new sales volume of *12,175 units*.

I now wish to present the second suggestion.

The Production Director came to see me. Following work study meetings, he told me that by altering production sequences he can *make substantial labour cost savings, although there will be an increase of approximately 10 per cent in fixed plant and machinery costs*.

Again – how will this affect company profitability?

Using the new production sequence, I have estimated a revised labour cost. The new total variable costs per unit will be:

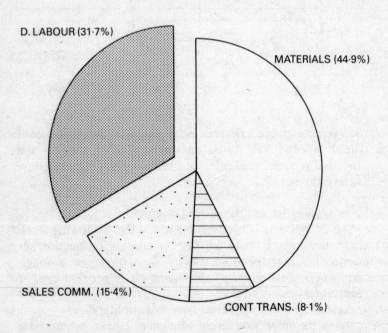

SLIDE 9

materials	£3.50	
cont. transport	£0.63	
sales commission	£1.20	
revised direct labour	£2.47	
TOTAL	£7.80	(40% of product sale price)

and graphically:

VARIABLE COSTS

D. LABOUR (31·7%)

MATERIALS (44·9%)

SALES COMM. (15·4%)

CONT TRANS. (8·1%)

Labour costs are now down to 31.7 per cent and the new fixed costs:

office/admin. costs	£42,570
marketing	£ 5,000
other overheads	£ 8,430
revised fixed plant & machinery	£15,400 (up 10%)
TOTAL	£71,400

and, graphically:

FIXED COSTS

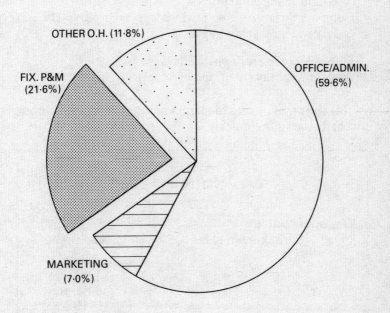

Now I will construct a table based on volume as before:

TABLE 3

Fixed costs		£71,400				
Variable costs as % sales		40				
Unit sale price		£19.50				

Units sold	0	2,000	4,000	6,000	8,000	10,000
Sales	£0	£39,000	£78,000	£117,000	£156,000	£195,000
Variable costs	£0	£15,600	£31,200	£46,800	£62,400	£78,000
Gross profit	£0	£23,400	£46,800	£70,200	£93,600	£117,000
Fixed costs	£71,400	£71,400	£71,400	£71,400	£71,400	£71,400
Net profit	(£71,400)	(£48,000)	(£24,600)	(£1,200)	£22,200	£45,600
Gross profit %	0%	60%	60%	60%	60%	60%
Total costs	£71,400	£87,000	£102,600	£118,200	£133,800	£149,400

Now this *is* an improvement!

We now break even at just over 6,000 units and at 8,000 to 10,000 units make good profits.

Compare this with Table 1, which shows our present break-even level. (Show Table 1 again.)

Our profitability is dramatically improved.
And, graphically (*see graph opposite*):

This shows an increased margin of safety, with break-even reached much more quickly.

SLIDE 11

Using our formula:

$$\text{Break-even sales} = \frac{\text{Fixed costs}}{\text{g.p.\%}}$$

$$= \frac{71,400}{60\%}$$

$$= £119,000$$

(or 6,102 units)

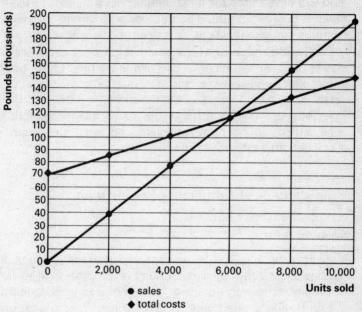

COMPANY 'A' PROFILE
F.C. £71·4 K–V.C. 40% – PRICE £19·50

- sales
- total costs

Our original quota was –

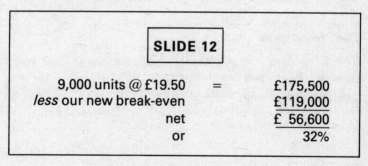

SLIDE 12		
9,000 units @ £19.50	=	£175,500
less our new break-even		£119,000
net		£ 56,600
or		32%

In conclusion, I feel that this second suggestion is worthy of further consideration and I recommend it to you . . .

Case-study Comments

You will have noted the large number of visual aids I used to make this presentation. The purpose was to put over some complex mathematical data in a clear and concise manner.

Each slide, table or graph could require an exchange of views, but you will have to be flexible on this. Quite often points which you are expecting to be queried are not, and vice versa!

As you are talking through the visual aids, your talk is 'guaranteed' to be more effective and keep the Board's continued interest and attention.

Case-study 2 – A Conference Presentation

Scenario

You have been asked to prepare and present a paper on 'Business Strategy' at a conference of engineers who are obviously technically qualified, but will be interested in learning more about other aspects of business. You are experienced in business and have additional financial skills.

The audience will be of around eighty to a hundred, and your talk is to last one hour. You have the knowledge to give such a talk, *but can you present it effectively?*

The Presentation

Thank you for the introduction, Mr Chairman . . . good morning, ladies and gentlemen.

I have been asked to talk on 'Business Strategy', and within the time available I would like to present to you *six key areas* for consideration (*slide 1*).

I want to begin with *business objectives*. Ask yourselves as business persons the following questions (*slide 2*).

SLIDE 1

Business Objectives

Management Responsibilities and Organisation

Product Marketing/Sales Targets

Production/Production Capacity

Product Pricing

Stock Control/Purchase Control

SLIDE 2

- Have you developed clear objectives, both short- and long-term?
- Are these objectives quantified in terms of market share, growth, product mix and rate of return?
- Have you built in review periods for your objectives, and can you be flexible?
- Have you developed financial and technical plans from these objectives?
- Are your objectives realistic?
- Don't forget high turnover is not necessarily the final answer. Are you profitable?
- Have you considered the significance of your objectives relative to your capital base?
- Have you analysed both the strengths *and* weaknesses of your business?
- Have you analysed management expertise?
- Have you identified the limiting factors to your business?

Objectives will vary greatly from one business to another. Objectives might be:

SLIDE 3

- high profit
- employment
- self-esteem
- succession

- to make a million
- a big car
- market share

Your objectives may be long-term or short-term. I think a good way of clarifying thoughts is to set them down on paper.

In considering the development of your objectives, limitations may include:

SLIDE 4

- your product
- the size of the market
- production capacity
- availability of raw materials
- financial resources
- management expertise

Moreover, a consideration of business strengths and weaknesses will help in the formation of your objectives. Likely areas for investigation are:

> ### SLIDE 5
>
> - product life-cycle
> - market competition
> - market position
> - management expertise

Now I will give three examples of formularising objectives.

> ### SLIDE 6
>
> **Statement of Objectives and Strategy**
>
> 1. To extend ....
> 2. To establish ....
> 3. To develop ....
> 4. ....

> ### SLIDE 7
>
> **Statement of Medium-term Objectives**
>
> Within the framework of our objectives, our medium-term strategy is:
>
> | | | Review dates | |
> |---|---|---|---|
> | 1. | To establish .... | X | X |
> | 2. | To develop .... | X | X |
> | 3. | .... | X | X |
> | 4. | .... | X | X |

```
┌─────────────────────────────────────────────┐
│                 ┌──────────┐                  │
│                 │ SLIDE 8  │                  │
│                 └──────────┘                  │
│   Statement of Short-term Plan (Twelve Months)│
│                 and Action                    │
├─────────────────────────────────────────────┤
│    Plan                Action to be taken (dates)│
│                                               │
│  1. To develop.......... 1. ...............   │
│                         Responsibility:       │
│  2. To establish ........ 2. ...............  │
│                         Responsibility:       │
│  3. ................... 3. ...............     │
│                         Responsibility:       │
│  4. ................... 4. ...............     │
└─────────────────────────────────────────────┘
```

What are the advantages of setting objectives? The advantages are:

```
┌─────────────────────────────────────────────┐
│                 ┌──────────┐                  │
│                 │ SLIDE 9  │                  │
│                 └──────────┘                  │
│                                               │
│    • clarification of objectives              │
│    • establishing a link between strategy and │
│      action plans                             │
│    • providing a framework for management/    │
│      department action                        │
│    • creating an involvement for management   │
│      by setting objectives and accountability │
│    • creating a motivating tool               │
│                                               │
└─────────────────────────────────────────────┘
```

The accent on *management* in Slide 9 leads us on to look at *management responsibilities and organisation*. Again, some questions to ask:

- Do you have an organisational chart?
- Are there gaps in key areas of management, general management, sales, production, finance or personnel?
- Do you have recruitment, training and promotion plans?
- Can your management team cope with expansion of the business?
- Is each job clearly defined?
- Have you delegated routine tasks as far as possible?
- Are managers accountable for specific areas of responsibility?
- Are there clearly defined lines of reporting?
- Do you co-ordinate projects with a team responsibility?

In a start-up situation, quite often the proprietor will be sales- or technically-orientated. It is important that he or she acquires accountancy/financial know-how, or builds up a team which includes such specialised skills.

Obviously, the larger the business, the more complex planning will become. An initial 'team' with expertise in the management of finance, sales, technology and accounts may not have sufficient depth if sales turnover grows into millions of pounds. Various areas of activity will need to be considered, such as personnel records, recruitment, selection, training, appraisal, career planning and management succession.

The business/corporate objectives discussed earlier will affect personnel planning both current and future. Management of departmental staffs must be aware of the need for accountability as a development of the business objectives.

Here is a typical company organisational chart:

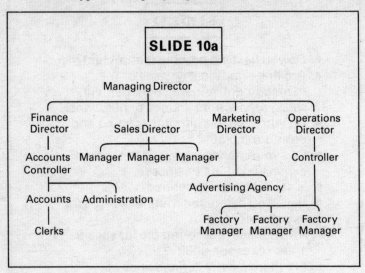

And, next, a job description form:

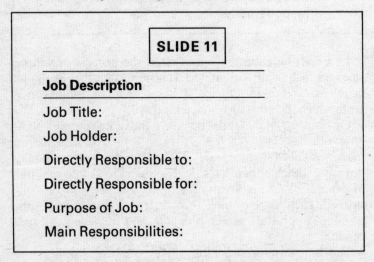

Dealing with recruitment and ongoing staff appraisal, you could use:

SLIDE 12

Individual Appraisal Assessment Form

Name: *Age:*

Job Position:

Appearance/Impact:

Intelligence/Qualifications:

Training History:

Responsibility Areas:

Other Abilities/Comments:

At this stage, let us recap. We have discussed objectives and management; what about the *company products*?

SLIDE 13

- Have you established the main factors affecting demand for your products, for example, market competition, prices, quantity, seasonability trends?
- Are your product lines expanding?
- Do you plan and research for follow-on products?
- Do you have a well-spread customer base?
- Do you monitor sales goods returned as defective?
- Do you review make or buy-in decisions?
- Have you defined specific sales areas and set sales targets?

Developing a marketing plan and committing this to paper in quantifiable terms is an essential follow-on from the business objectives we looked at earlier. By producing a plan containing targets for achievement within a coming period (usually twelve months), a standard is set against which performance can be measured.

In studying the market-place, the business will benefit from an appraisal including market competition and market needs. Looking at existing products will help one to perceive the pattern of sales, as well as possible new product development to follow on from existing products.

Promotion of products can be carried out in differing ways:

SLIDE 14

- media advertising
- the promotional package
- field personnel
- direct mail
- telephone sales

In order to monitor cost-effectiveness, a promotional budget should be set up, and the ratio of costs to sales generated should be monitored.

Businesses need to know volumes of products sold: in which areas; by which salesman; to which customer.

The use of coding on sales invoices is the usual method to aid analysis, and a monthly check on results is normally adequate unless very high volumes are involved.

SLIDE 15

Sales Analysis by Product Group

Month ended:

Product group	Sales value		
	This period £	*Year to date £*	*Previous year £*
Total sales			

SLIDE 16

Sales Analysis by Area Salesman

Month ended:

Area salesman	Sales value £
Total sales	

Moving on to the *production* area – with an audience of technical engineers knowing far more about it than I do – I would just pose the following points for consideration:

SLIDE 17

- Do you plan production levels to link in with exports and sales?
- If sales are made from finished goods stock, do you control lead times correctly?
- Does your business have the physical production capability to meet planned sales?
- Are the premises adequate?
- Do you have job cards setting out raw material requirements and estimating labour/machine hours for specific products?
- Do you plan for effective production runs rather than piecework?
- Do you monitor labour efficiency?
- Does your production controller liaise with your buyer to ensure an adequate, but not excessive raw material stock?
- Do you monitor wastage of materials?
- Do you monitor defective goods returned?

Managing production is concerned with managing the physical resources of the business as efficiently as possible so as to create the products necessary to meet the marketing demand.

Production efficiency is *very* important. A high proportion of manufacturing business's costs will be tied into production, for example:

SLIDE 18

- direct wages
- materials
- shop-floor machinery (capital costs and running costs)

No matter how well a job is estimated on a cost of materials and work-hours basis, if the production in terms of labour/materials usage efficiency is poor, then the *true* cost of the finished articles will be off-budget.

Production can be thought of as the management of:

SLIDE 19

- design/layout of production

- scheduling and controlling of production

- labour management

- materials management

- quality control

Make or buy-in decisions will need to be made on a number of items, and generally the decision will be made on a cost-effectiveness basis.

Now I want to move on to *product pricing* – a sensitive area.

The setting of the 'right' price for the product is one of the most difficult judgement areas in business. The right price for profitability may not necessarily be the price the market-place will accept. Price-setting based on careful costings plus a mark-up for profit tends to be most widely used in business.

However, there are also many situations in which price is dictated by competition and/or demand, for example, in tenders for contract.

Let me ask:

SLIDE 20

- Are costs estimated first to give a guide-line to the price-setters?
- Are you careful in the giving of discounts for large orders or early payment?
- Are you careful to calculate the true 'cost' of discounts?
- Does your cost estimate include an element for future inflation?
- Do you price at the highest level acceptable in the market-place?
- Do you endeavour to find out what your competitors are charging?
- Have you established a minimum price for your product to achieve break-even?
- Are there certain elements of products where you would be better off buying-in rather than making?
- Do you frequently review prices?
- Do you undertake market research?

Moving into the final part of this session, I want to discuss *stock control and purchase control*, two key areas of business.

The areas of stock control and purchase control are obviously very closely related and can be considered together as materials management. This is a very important area for both manufacturing and retailing businesses; both will spend a high proportion of their anticipated sales income on the

- Do you know the lead time for your products?
- Are stocks kept to a minimum acceptable level for operational needs?
- Pareto's principle, or the 80/20 rule, can be useful in stock control; that is, does 20 per cent of your stock articles represent 80 per cent of the total stock value?
- Do you have an effective stock-control system?
- Do you carry out quarterly physical stock-taking as a measure of control?
- Do you have a monthly review of stock holding?
- Do you frequently get quotes from new suppliers to check on purchasing prices?
- Can suppliers carry stock and make more frequent delivery to you?
- Are you careful not to buy in large quantities just to obtain a discount?
- Do you have separate stock-level guides for raw materials/work in progress and finished goods?
- Do you dispose of obsolete stock?
- Are you insured?

purchase of materials from outside organisations. Locking a business into one particular supplier possibly could be dangerous from the aspect of supply availability. Material management involves not only the management of sufficient materials available to meet production time schedules, but also the management of the general stock level holding – much capital can be tied up in stock holding.

SLIDE 22

Order Form

Order _Work Sheet No._

Company Name _Customer Order No._

Address _Date_

Contact Name and Title _Tel. No._

Item	_Description_	_Date ordered_	_Delivery date_

Quotation Number:

Materials/stock

Items	_Ordered from_	_Ordered by_	_Delivered by_

Instructions as per quote: Technical _Quote time_

Instructions to packing

Instructions (Miscellaneous)

Packing and delivery to:

It is advisable to review materials purchasing on a regular basis, to obtain quotes from alternative suppliers, and also to seek discounts where available. A word of caution on discounts: it is important to evaluate 'the true cost' of carrying additional stock through bulk buyings against the benefit of a discount on a larger order.

Here is an example of an order form (opposite page).

– and another:

SLIDE 23

Purchase Requisition

Date: *Department:*

Supplier Nominated:

Quantity and Description of Item(s):

Price:

Date Required:

Requisitioned by:

Authorised by:

And now for stock control.

The whole area of stock control is one of conflicting interests. While businesses do not wish to run the danger of stock-outs, the purpose of stock control is to endeavour to find a balance between the benefit of holding stocks, weighed against the disadvantage of having capital tied up in stock, which will mean that less capital is available for other purposes. Also there is the danger that stock will deteriorate or become obsolete. In retailing, for example, the holding of 'fashionable' products may lead to quick obsolescence. Skateboards provide a good example; they were very fashionable a few years ago, their popularity dwindled rapidly – now children seem to favour roller skates once more, only this time, roller boots!

In manufacturing, of course, stock holding comprises not just basic materials but a mixture of raw materials and components, work in progress and finished goods. It is therefore important to carry out analysis of manufacturing stock.

SLIDE 24		
Analysis of Manufacturing Stock		
Month ended:		
Stock	*£*	*As a percentage*
Raw materials		
Work in progress		
Finished goods		
Total stock		

The value of work in progress will vary enormously between different types of industrial manufacturer. Also, efficiency within the factory will dictate the product production-cycle period, which will in turn affect the overall amount of capital tied up in work in progress as opposed to finished goods.

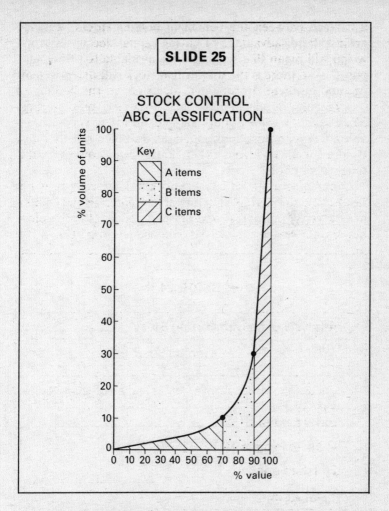

The basis of this ABC classification is that the A items, which represent 70 per cent of the total stock value in numerical terms, only represent 10 per cent of the total volume of the units held in stock. For this reason the greatest measure of control and attention can be afforded to the A items, with secondary attention being given to those classified as B items.

Stock-taking, particularly in manufacturing business, can be a very tedious and time-consuming chore. However, it is obviously very important to evaluate the quantity of stock and materials and work in progress on hand. Certainly for the annual audit stocks should be checked, and at the same time the opportunity should be taken to review obsolete and redundant stocks.

SLIDE 26

Stock Count

Category	Value £
Total	

In conclusion, Mr Chairman, ladies and gentlemen, let me reshow my first slide:

SLIDE 1

Business Objectives

Management Responsibilities and Organisation

Product Marketing/Sales Targets

Production/Production Capacity

Product Pricing

Stock Control/Purchase Control

Today we have examined six key areas of *business strategy –
I hope it has proved of benefit for you. Thank you for your
attention.*

Case-study Comments

A difficult and complex subject in a large audience setting.
Careful preparation backed up by clear visual aids will,
however, make it enjoyable to present and a pleasure for your
audience!

Case-study 3 – A Group-leading Session

Scenario

You are a group leader at a training centre. You have a
thirty-minute slot on *Break-even Analysis*. The twelve students in the group all have a reasonable working knowledge of
accountancy *but*, as with all students, you need to get them
involved! Your style will be much more relaxed and you must
encourage discussion.

Your delivery narrative will be only key-words backed by
acetates.

The Presentation

BREAK-EVEN ANALYSIS   OVERHEAD
                                       PROJECTOR

1.   Outline topic – key areas.   Slide 1

SALES

less VARIABLE COSTS

= CONTRIBUTION

less FIXED COSTS

= NET PROFIT

2.   Define break-even point.   Slide 2

> POINT AT WHICH INCOME
>
> MEETS EXPENDITURE

3.   Ask group for a formula.

4.   Give formula to be written down.   Slide 3

$$B.E. = \frac{F.C.}{P.V.}$$

5.   Give out exercise – allow fifteen minutes.

EXERCISE: COMPANIES A & B

	Co. A.	Co. B.
	(£000)	
SALES	300	500
VARIABLE COSTS	80	375
CONTRIBUTION	220	125
FIXED COSTS	190	75
NET PROFIT	30	50
RETURN ON SALES	10%	10%
P.V. RATIO	.73	.25

Required

(i) Calculate break-even point on both companies.

(ii) Which company would be most adversely affected by a 20 per cent reduction in sales?

6. Obtain answers verbally.

7. Run through answers.

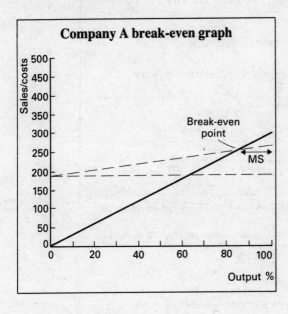

Company A break-even graph

$$B.E. = \frac{F.C.}{P.V.} = \frac{190}{.73}$$

$$= 260,000$$

Slide 5

97

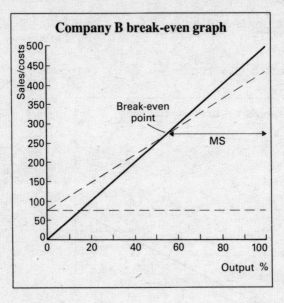

$$B.E. = \frac{F.C.}{P.V.} = \frac{75}{.25}$$

$$= 300,000$$

20% REDUCTION IN SALES

	Co. A	Co. B
	(£000)	
NEW SALES	240	400
NEW VARIABLE COSTS	64	300
CONTRIBUTION	176	100
FIXED COST	190	75
NET PROFIT	(14)	25

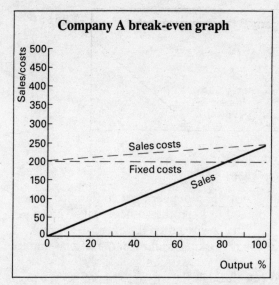

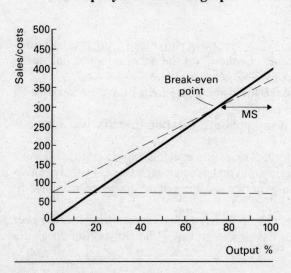

Company B break-even graph

$$B.E. = \frac{F.C.}{P.V.}$$

$$= \frac{75}{.25}$$

$$= 300,000$$

Case-study Comments

A less demanding task than delivering a conference paper! However, you do need to keep the students involved to get continued interest. That's why I used the exercise to break up the talk and get them working while I had a fifteen-minute rest!

Take time to run through the answer. Make good use of the overhead projector to make your presentation more effective.

A Positive Close

This is perhaps the most powerful aid to your presentation. Very dependent, of course, on the occasion – but imagine a conference. A suitable close could be:

'In conclusion ladies and gentlemen I have reviewed with you the key areas of . . .

It has been my pleasure to attend; thank you for your attention.'

Whatever style of close you use, it is important to leave your audience certain that you have in fact *finished*. With a positive close you can generate an immediate audience response to your talk.

I remember one of the best talks (in my opinion) that I ever presented fell flat at the end as I did not bother to give a positive close!

Questions

In group training and small groups you should encourage questions as you go along. This adds variety and keeps the participants involved.

In a conference questions will usually come at the end. If there are several speakers then an open forum is often adopted and you should find this type of question time easy enough to handle provided you're familiar with your subject material.

The most difficult situation is in conference as a single speaker. Question time will certainly test you. The number of questions seems unpredictable – occasionally you don't get any at all!

You need to think quickly – formulate short responses rather than entering into lengthy debate. If the question is beyond the scope of your talk, then don't be afraid to say so.

My last notes take the form of a short Postscript – 'things that can go wrong' . . . despite all our comprehensive planning and *preparation*.

6   Postscript

Things That Can Go Wrong

Example 1

Remember my first talk to a small group and the difficulties with the whiteboard lay-out and the incorrect timing of the hand-out causing people to sit and read this while I moved on to fresh material. Room lay-out and timing can be crucial.

Example 2

The venue was a hotel with a room big enough for the expected audience of around a hundred. I was the only speaker and I had checked by telephone the room lay-out and availability of visual aids. The organiser assured me that there was a screen for the overhead projector. Imagine my horror when on arrival the screen was so minute there was no way it could be viewed from the middle or the back of the room. We had to improvise by hanging up a large white tablecloth!

Example 3

I arrived in a small town. The venue a small room in a small hotel. My presentation included the use of video. The organiser had assured me that facilities were available. In fact it was a mismatch of the hotel TV and someone's home video! I could not get it tuned in but fortunately we caught a local TV man just before his shop closed at 6 p.m.

Example 4

The talk mentioned above in Example 3 went well despite the technical hitch, and by chance the next night I was speaking again, this time in a large city to an audience of 120 who I anticipated would be a much more sophisticated group. The journey was a long one, so I went by train and took the opportunity to rescript my talk during the journey.

I had no opportunity therefore to *speak the words aloud*, and when I delivered the talk I stumbled my way through. So much for hoping to do well in front of this larger group!

Example 5

The meeting was with a small group but in a very large room with a platform elevated about 4 ft from the floor. Because it was such a small group I did not want the formality of speaking from this high platform and wished to work from the floor near to the audience. I needed to use the overhead projector but the electrical cable could not be arranged to reach where I was standing. The compromise was that if I stood on the floor, with the overhead projector on the platform, then the organiser would put on and take off the slides. This probably sounds OK in theory. However, it was a disaster in practice with slides whisked on and off and out of sequence with the talk!

I hope you enjoy your presentations and this book helps you to give them more *effectively*.

Appendix: Talk Checklist

date _____

venue _____

directions _____

_____

topic _____

visual aids _____

audience size and experience _____

_____

room layout and size _____

other speakers _____

length of talk _____

and time to commence _____

fee _____